ISBN 978-1-333-40374-4
PIBN 10500210

1 MONTH OF
FREE
READING

at

www.ForgottenBooks.com

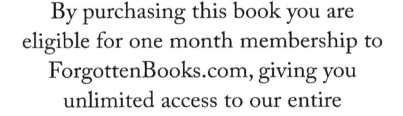

By purchasing this book you are eligible for one month membership to ForgottenBooks.com, giving you unlimited access to our entire collection of over 1,000,000 titles via our web site and mobile apps.

To claim your free month visit:
www.forgottenbooks.com/free500210

English
Français
Deutsche
Italiano
Español
Português

www.forgottenbooks.com

Mythology Photography **Fiction**
Fishing Christianity **Art** Cooking
Essays Buddhism Freemasonry
Medicine **Biology** Music **Ancient
Egypt** Evolution Carpentry Physics
Dance Geology **Mathematics** Fitness
Shakespeare **Folklore** Yoga Marketing
Confidence Immortality Biographies
Poetry **Psychology** Witchcraft
Electronics Chemistry History **Law**
Accounting **Philosophy** Anthropology
Alchemy Drama Quantum Mechanics
Atheism Sexual Health **Ancient History**
Entrepreneurship Languages Sport
Paleontology Needlework Islam
Metaphysics Investment Archaeology
Parenting Statistics Criminology
Motivational

FREMONT'S HUNDRED DAYS IN MISSOURI.

SPEECH OF SCHUYLER COLFAX,

OF INDIANA,

1823-1885

IN REPLY TO MR. BLAIR, OF MISSOURI,

DELIVERED

In the House of Representatives, March 7, 1862.

The House being in Committee of the Whole on the state of the Union—

Mr. COLFAX said: Mr. Chairman, I did not intend, at the opening of my friend's remarks, to speak on this subject to-day; and therefore am but illy prepared to answer his elaborate argument of two hours in length. But I am gratified that the House, on my motion, extended his time, so that he could present the whole array of charges at once.

While I differed, as is known to him and many other members of the House, with the Administration, which I assisted to elect, as to the supersedure of Major General Fremont in the department of the West, I desire, lest I might be misunderstood, to say at the outset, once and for all, that no matter what general the Administration may put up or put down, I shall sustain it with all my heart and soul and strength and mind in every military movement that it makes against the enemy. I believe it to be our duty to do so. It is, under God, the only means by which we can put down this gigantic, satanic, conspiracy and rebellion. And although I lament the supersedure of a general who lives to-day in the loyal hearts of millions of the American people, that can make no difference in my earnest and cordial support of the Administration.

I pass over many remarks of the gentleman from Missouri, [Mr. BLAIR,] which, I am sure, he will himself, in his cooler moments, regret. He has seen fit to mingle personalities with his criticisms, and to speak of a gentleman who holds a commission as major general in the army as a tool, a dupe, a designing man. I cannot follow the gentleman here. The subject is too grave to be thus discussed.

There has been a warm friendship between myself and the gentleman from Missouri almost since our boyhood, and I shall not suffer a single remark to fall from my lips which could wound him or any friend of his, or any member of his family. I rise simply to vindicate history, and to prove, from the records of the day, that my friend from Missouri has had his feelings and judgment perverted, or, perhaps, I should rather say influenced, by prejudice. He spoke about the "idolators" of Fremont. My friend has not used the word fittingly. Those whom he calls the idolators of Fremont are the men who stand by him to-day, just as my friend did from the commencement of his acquaintance with him till the last of August, 1861, up to which time he was his warm, his devoted friend and admirer. He ought, from that long acquaintance, to have known his mind, his capacity, his judgment, his will. In August he was his friend, warm and true; in September he was not. All my crime is, that I continue the same friendship that, in common with him, I had in August, and did not change with him in September.

Mr. Chairman, men are but nothing in this struggle. They are but ciphers—the whole of them. These generals, with all their epaulets and sashes, are but the instruments by which the strong arm of the country is to put down this rebellion. Since the war broke out, I have, in my humble sphere and capacity, endeavored to preach the doctrine of forbearance and concord and unity, and have implored men on all sides to cease depreciating our generals. I have said that when they go forth at the head of their armies with their lives in their hands, they are entitled to confidence and respect. When the Administration supersedes them, well and good; let them pass away, unless, so far as, this afternoon, we vindicate the past, without saying what the Administration shall do in the future. I say this as to General McClellan, as I do about General Fremont, and every other general commanding. Whether the Administration shall yield to the wishes of hosts of the people by giving General Fremont another command, is no part of my argument to-day. I have no right to dictate on this point; and further than I have already advised, I shall say nothing.

I have this, also, to say about General Fremont; I do not take him to be perfect. I know that all 'men' are 'fallible. 'He is sometimes an impulsive man. He has feelings, like all of us who are made of flesh and blood. I regret very much that he suffered this publication to be made, which the chairman of the joint committee on the conduct of the war objected to to-day. I wish that he had bided his time a little longer. For six months he has been standing with closed lips, and listening to the allegations against him with a reticence which has commanded the approbation not only of his friends at home, but of thousands elsewhere in the civilized world, waiting patiently for the hour of his vindication. I wish he could have waited a few days longer. But I think that something ought to be pardoned to a man who had poisoned arrows hurled against him from every side, and who had been deposed from his command under circumstances so painful and trying.

Without disparaging any other general, I have this also to say of General Fremont: he is the only major general of the army who has, in this war, up to this date, gone out with his troops, away from his headquarters—gone out over field and valley and mountain and plain and river. He was the only one. I suppose the others are willing to do it. But while that record lives—and it will live in history—no man will believe the intimations of the gentleman from Missouri, that Fremont is a timid man. The schoolboy at the log school-house knows very well that there is not a particle of timidity about the man. He may or may not have been fitted for the command of the department of the West. I sincerely think he was. But whether he was or not, he is a brave and fearless man. He has braved death in a thousand forms, and has written his name high up on the scroll of history as a great discoverer, or as a great adventurer, if you will. He has planted the Stars and Stripes on the highest point of the Rocky Mountains. He has suffered privation and suffering and toil in his daring journeys. His cheek has not blanched in the presence of danger or of death. And when he knew that the sword of Damocles was hanging over his head by a single hair, he went forth with his army in pursuit of the enemy, to punish treason with the sword, and encamped with the advance guard, instead of with the rear, as is usually the custom of commanding generals. No, sir; General Fremont is not a coward. He has no timidity.

Mr. BLAIR, of Missouri. My friend does not state, I trust, that I called General Fremont a coward.

Mr. COLFAX. The language that my friend used was "timidity," which is of course a qualified degree of cowardice.

Now, in relation to this contract for the construction of earthworks in St. Louis, I wish to say that I will be frank upon this subject as upon every other. I do not approve of that contract. I think the contractor made too much money out of it. I do not suppose it was made upon the judgment of General Fremont, but that he yielded to the opinions of the heads of the engineer department about prices. I think the prices were too high, and truth compels me to say so, because, when I stand here to vindicate General Fremont, I will not sacrifice the truth to vindicate him or anybody else. If I speak at all, I must express my convictions. But admitting that there was extravagance in his department, I ask whether every other department of the army has been managed with more care and less extravagance? Has not the Government been imposed on even here, despite the keenest watchfulness of the most experienced officers, some of whom have had no military duties to engross or distract their minds?

Adj. Gen. Thomas says in his report that two or three hundred horses were found unfit for service; that they were lame and ringboned and spavined, although it is not proved that Fremont had seen a single one of them. Well, sir, when I came to Washington at the beginning of the present session, upon looking into the Star, I noticed the sale of fourteen hundred condemned Government horses, of the army of the Potomac, which brought prices ranging from twenty-five cents to sixty dollars. Yet my friend had no denunciations against the management of this department. In time of war, in conducting operations on so extensive a scale, the experience of England in the Crimean war, and of all other nations at such times, unfortunately prove that it is not to be expected that everything would be precisely right, that all articles shall be suddenly bought of the best quality and at the lowest prices. I noticed, also, that the exhibits attached to General Thomas's report contained two singular complaints against General Fremont. One was a complaint by General Hunter, that Fremont had ordered him into the field, and that he had forty wagons and only forty-one mules. And the very next of the exhibits was a complaint by Quartermaster Turnley, within a few days of the date of General Hunter's letter, complaining that Fremont had ordered him to push on the inspection of mules as rapidly as possible. I think these two complaints exactly answer each other. But how could Fremont have satisfied both critics?

My friend from Missouri vindicates the character of the city of St. Louis. I wish I could believe all he says about the loyalty of that city, for I think it is a very pleasant city. I have spent many pleasant days there; I have enjoyed not only the hospitality of my friend from Missouri, representing the St. Louis district, but of many other friends in that city. I believe with him that the great body of the working men of that city are loyal, but that a majority of the men of wealth and high social position there are disloyal.

Mr. BLAIR, of Missouri. The gentleman is mistaken.

Mr. COLFAX. I cannot yield to my friend, at least until I have finished this sentence. Why, sir, even since General Halleck assumed the command of that department the secession candidates for officers of the Chamber of Commerce of St. Louis were elected by a sweeping majority.

Mr. BLAIR, of Missouri. It is true that the secession candidates were elected by the Chamber of Commerce by a majority, and the same fact is true in reference to the Mercantile Library Association of St. Louis, but that only shows that the commercial men of the city were largely engaged in commerce with the South, and were in that way identified with secession. But I say to the gentleman that I know the city well, and I know that the two regiments raised, which General Lyon took prisoners at Camp Jackson, were all the secession troops they could raise, and all they could arm. There was never any necessity of declaring martial law.

Mr. COLFAX. I beg to say to my friend that I know something about St. Louis, though not, of course, as much as himself. I have not only visited it frequently, but I read the newspapers published there, and particularly a paper which used to be considered his organ, but I believe is not now a favorite of his, the St. Louis *Democrat*. And my friend knows very well that in the case of the Mercantile Library Association, every effort was made, both by the Unionists and secessionists, to carry the election; that the Union men paid the dues of Union members in arrears, and proposed numbers of others, qualified for admission, for the purpose of obtaining their votes, but nevertheless were defeated by a large majority.

Mr. BLAIR, of Missouri. The reason why the Union men left the Hall, and refused to participate in the meeting, was, that a hundred Union candidates to become members were excluded by a majority of the old members, under a technical rule requiring one day's notice before admission. I do not often read the organ of the Fremont party, of which the gentleman speaks, but I think I am pretty well acquainted with the facts, nevertheless.

Mr. COLFAX. I have no doubt of it, and my friend knows very well that these members of the Chamber of Commerce, who elected their secession candidate, voted for him openly as such in face of the United States military authorities in the city. They made no professions of zealous loyalty, as many secessionists have done in face of an armed force. Their conduct was so open and undisguised that General Halleck ordered every one of the officers elect to come up and take the oath of allegiance; being, I believe, the first civilians he imposed this upon, though he has required since more extensively still.

Mr. BLAIR, of Missouri. The gentleman will allow me to say——

Mr. COLFAX. I cannot yield further. I did not interrupt my friend the whole time he was speaking.

Mr. BLAIR, of Missouri. The gentleman says they were openly secession——

The CHAIRMAN. The gentleman from Missouri is out of order. The gentleman from Indiana declines to yield.

Mr. BLAIR, of Missouri. I am a little sensitive upon this point.

Mr. COLFAX. Then I will yield, of course.

Mr. BLAIR, of Missouri. I merely desire to say that these men did not vote for what was called a secession candidate, but for a man known to be a Union man, and who refused to hold the office after he had been elected.

Mr. COLFAX. Still the statement remains uncontradicted that he was voted for as a secession candidate by those who sympathized with the men who are in arms against the Government, and was elected as such.

Mr. Chairman, I know that the mass of the people of the city of St. Louis, the working people, as I said previously, are loyal; for, sir, when this same General Fremont came back to that city after his removal; when he came with no favors to confer, but degraded, dishonored, deposed from his command, the loyal people of that city, who had heard all the charges of their Representative against him, but who still confided in him, flocked by thousands and tens of thousands, with banners and torchlights, and music and shoutings, to welcome him as no man was ever welcomed there before. Oh, yes, sir, the heart of the people of St. Louis is loyal; they have proved it so.

RESPONSIBILITY FOR THE DEATH OF GENERAL LYON.

My friend from St. Louis has quoted documents and presented arguments to prove that General Fremont had it in his power to reinforce General Lyon before the battle of Springfield, and that his failure to perform that duty was the cause of General Lyon's death, and these I desire now to examine. Sir, the death of General Lyon occurred on the 10th of August, and yet the friendship of the gentleman from Missouri for General Fremont continued undiminished for weeks after. He continued to be the friend of the man whom he now arraigns as a guilty criminal; for if the charges he makes are proved, General Fremont, in wilfully suffering the death of that gallant officer, was guilty of a no less crime than murder. I think I can show to this committee that twenty days after the death of General Lyon my friend from Missouri did not charge General Fremont with crime in failing to send reinforcements. I will read the dispatch of Captain Schofield, now General Schofield, whom my friend knows; because he was, I believe, connected with his regiment at St. Louis when

I was there. I want to show the reasons why General Lyon was not reinforced, and I shall show it in a way my friend from Missouri cannot deny, unless he denies the documents themselves. In his dispatch, as adjutant general of General Lyon, dated Springfield, July 15, he says :

"Governor Jackson is concentrating his forces in the southwestern part of the State, and is receiving large reinforcements from Arkansas, Tennessee, Louisiana, and Texas. His effective force will soon be certainly not less than thirty thousand men, probably much larger. *All idea of any further advance movement, or of even maintaining our present position, must soon be abandoned, unless the Government furnish us promptly with large reinforcements and supplies.* Our troops are badly clothed, poorly fed, and imperfectly supplied with tents ; none of them have yet been paid, and the three months' volunteers have become disheartened to such an extent that very few of them are willing to renew their enlistment. The blank pay-rolls are not here, and the long time required to get them here, fill them up, send them to Washington, have the payment ordered, and the pay-master reach us, leaves us no hope that our troops can be paid for five or six weeks to come. Upon these circumstances there remains no other course but to urgently press upon the attention of the Government the absolute necessity of sending us fresh troops at once, with ample supplies for them and for those now here. At least ten thousand men should be sent, and that promptly. *You will send the inclosed despatch by telegraph to General McClellan, and also to the War Department,* and forward by mail a copy of this letter."

This is directed to Chester Harding, jr., assistant adjutant general at St. Louis, who doubtless sent the dispatch to General McClellan as requested, and here is the dispatch, dated July 20, of General McClellan, in reply :

To CHESTER HARDING, Jr, *Assistant Adjutant General :*
In case of an attack on Cairo, have none but Illinois troops to reinforce, and only eleven thousand arms in Illinois. Will direct two regiments to be ready at Caseyville ; but you will only use them for defence of St. Louis, and in case of absolute necessity. Telegraph me from time to time.
G. B. McCLELLAN,
Major General United States Army.

He could not allow reinforcements to go to the support of General Lyon in the southwest. There was more imminent danger he felt nearer by; and he pointed to Cairo as one of the threatened points, and St. Louis as another. He will "direct two regiments to be ready at Caseyville, but you will ONLY use them for defence of St. Louis, and in case of absolute necessity." Here is a dispatch of General McClellan, five days after Lyon's appeal for troops through his assistant adjutant general, and six days before General Fremont arrived at St. Louis, declining to send reinforcements to General Lyon. And now I want General Lyon to speak from his grave, and answer whether he considers General Fremont responsible for his death.

I read, first, a letter from Lyon himself to Assistant Adjutant General Harding, at St. Louis:

SPRINGFIELD, MISSOURI, *July 17, 1861.*
SIR: I inclose you a copy of a letter to Col. Townsend on the subject of an order from Gen. Scott, which calls for five companies of the second infantry *to be withdrawn from the West and sent to Washington. A previous order withdraws the mounted troops,* as I am informed, and were it not that some of them were *en route* to this place they would now be in Washington. *This order carried out would not now leave at Fort Leavenworth a single company. I have companies B and E second infantry now under orders for Washington, and if all these troops leave me I can do nothing, and must retire in the absence of other troops to supply their places.* In fact, I am badly enough off at the

best, and must utterly fail if my regulars all go. At Washington troops from all the Northern, Middle, and Eastern States are available for the support of the army in Virginia, and more are understood to be already there than are wanted, and it seems strange that so many troops must go on from the West, *and strip us of the means of defence ; but if it is the intention to give up the West, let it be so.*

I omit a severe allusion to General Scott, because I do not wish, by reproducing it here, even to give it currency, feeling that General Lyon, in his great anxiety, did him injustice. The letter concludes :

Cannot you stir up this matter and secure us relief? See Fremont if he has arrived. The want of supplies has crippled me so that I cannot move, and I do not know when I can. Everything seems to combine against me at this point. Stir up Blair.
Yours truly,
N. LYON, *Commanding.*
Colonel HARDING, *St. Louis Arsenal, Missouri.*

I would not allude to my friend's brother at all if it had not been that he himself alluded to him in his speech, and the only allusion I shall have occasion to make to him is the one I am now about to make. I wish to use his evidence to show why General Lyon was not reinforced. On the 26th of July last, Montgomery Blair wrote to General Fremont as follows :

WASHINGTON, *July 26, 1861.*
DEAR GENERAL : I have two telegrams from you, but find it impossible now to get any attention to Missouri or Western matters from the authorities here. You will have to do the best you can, and take all needful responsibility to defend and protect the people over whom you are specially set. *   *   *   *   *   *   *   *
Yours, truly, and in haste,
M. BLAIR.

That was five days after the battle of Bull Run, and when this city was supposed to be in imminent danger ; and I doubt not that fact explains why the West was comparatively neglected. I shall assume that, and blame no one, for my object and resolution is to attack no one to-day, but to simply give reasons for the faith that is in me.

I shall read now some more extracts from General Lyon's correspondence, because the one I have read was not the only protest he made. The next is from a letter from General Lyon, written to Colonel Harding on the day after Fremont reached St. Louis, and ten days after the previous letter. He says, under date of July 27 :

"If the Government cannot give due attention to the West her interests must have a corresponding disparagement."

And in a memorandum from General Lyon, sent by Colonel Phelps to General Fremont, dated Springfield, July 27, he says :

"*The safety of the State is hazarded* ; orders from General Scott strip the entire West of regular forces, and increase the chances of sacrificing it."

But I wish now to read the statement of his assistant adjutant general, Colonel Harding. It is long, but it does justice to the dead general and to the living general ; and it is written by the assistant adjutant general, who, from his confidential relations with his chief, knew his thoughts best of all men now living.

"Looking, then, to the position of affairs in this State on the 26th July, 1861, it will be found that Gen. Lyon was in the southwest, in need of reinforcements. There was trouble in the northwest, requiring more troops than were there. In the northeast there were no more troops than were required to perform the task allotted to them, while in the south and southeast there was a rebel army of sufficient force to endanger Bird's Point, Cape Girardeau, Ironton, Rolla, and St. Louis, and no adequate preparation was made to meet it.

"Gen. Fremont sent the 8th Missouri to Cape Girardeau, and the 4th U. S. Reserve Corps (whose term of service was to expire on the 8th August) to reinforce Bland at Ironton. He took some of Gen. Pope's force from him, added to it two battalions of the 1st and 2d U. S. Reserve Corps, (whose term of service was to expire on the 7th August,) equipped Buel's light battery, and started about the 1st August for Bird's Point, with the troops thus collected, being something less than 3,800 men, and being also all the available troops in this region, expecting to find an enemy not less than 20,000 strong

"Subsequent events showed that the rebel force was not overestimated and nothing but the reinforcements sent to the points above named and the expedition down the river prevented its advance upon them Common report greatly magnified these reinforcements; and it was generally believed in the city, and no doubt so reported to the rebel leaders, that Fremont had moved some 10,000 or 12,000 troops to the southeast, while in fact he did not have over 5,500 to move, and was not strong enough at any point to take the field and commence offensive operations

"Gen. Fremont *was not* inattentive to the situation of Gen'. Lyon's column, and went so far as to remove the garrison of Booneville, in order to send him aid."

But my friend from Missouri says that there were quantities of troops coming into St. Louis who could have been detailed to reinforce General Lyon. So there were ; but hear what Colouel Harding says :

"During the first days of August, troops arrived in the city in large numbers. *Nearly all of them were unarmed ; all were without* transportation. *Regiment after regiment laid for days in the city without any equipments, for the reason that the arsenal was exhausted, and arms and accoutrements had to be brought from the East.* From these men General Lyon would have had reinforcements, although they were wholly unpracticed in the use of the musket, and knew nothing of movements in the field ; but in the mean time the battle of the 10th of August was fought."

And yet, when they were entirely without arms, and Fremont sought, at this very time—the 6th of August—in his overwhelming anxiety and solicitude, to buy any kind of arms to put into their hands to protect the Untou, and put down the rebellion, and save the lives of our brave soldiers and their generals at all the exposed points in his department, he was denounced from one end of the country to the other as being in the hands of contractors, and in corrupt collusion with knaves. The inferior arms that he bought at this critical moment—in his hour of direst extremity—forms one of the counts of the Investigating Committee's indictment against him. If this is justice, God save me from ever being in any position in this Government to receive such justice !

My friend stated, and I took down the exact words that fell from his lips, that "there was at that time no necessity to reinforce Cairo from St. Louis ; that it could have been reinforced from other directions." Now, I differ with him on that point, and I think I can prove that I am right. Fremont then had actually but little available force under his command. Indeed, on the 16th of July, only ten days before Fremont reached St. Louis, General Lyon had had to authorize one regiment of his little band at Springfield (Colonel Brown's fourth) to return

to St. Louis, to be mustered out of service, at the expiration of their three months' enlistment. The three months' men would not re-enlist, because they could not get their pay. The West at that time, in the pressure from the East, and the imminent peril of the Capital, seemed to be neglected. The troops already under arms did not see the paymaster, and they would not re-enlist. With this inadequate force and this lack of arms, Fremont had to choose between reinforcing one point or the other. Now, I submit the question to the House and the country, which of those two points was the most important; the one at the end of a wagon road in southwestern Missouri, whence Lyon could possibly retreat if he felt that he could not sustain his position, and the other at the mouth of the Ohio river, where it joins the Mississippi, commanding both streams, and the furthest point south of which we had possession? Which was the most important? Should they retire from Cairo or from Springfield? I contend, that, as this evidence proves, Fremont could only reinforce one of these points, and he went down to Cairo on the 1st of August. My friend insists that General Prentiss's dispatches prove that he did not stand in pressing need of reinforcements. Let us see. I read now what General Prentiss said. General Prentiss was commanding at Cairo, and on the 23d of July he wrote to Colonel Harding as follows :

"Have but eight (8) regiments here. *Six (6) of them are three (3) months' men Their time expires this week*—are reorganizing now. I have neither tents nor wagons, and must hold Cairo and Bird's Point."

He said he had but eight regiments, and six of them were three months' men, and their term expired that very week, before Fremont could get there, leaving only two certainly available regiments at Cairo. Now let us see what was the position of the rebel forces in the vicinity of Cairo. I read again from General Prentiss, under date of July 28 :

"To Major General FREMONT :

"Rebels from Tennessee are concentrating at New Madrid, Missouri, with avowed intention of assaulting Bird's Point. They may intend going to Cape Girardeau. Colonel Marsh has no battery. *I have none to spare. My command is merging from three months' to three years' service on half recess.* Mustering in yesterday and to-day. *I have but two six-pounders prepared to move.*"

We come down now to July 29, the next day. General Prentiss again telegraphs Fremont; and you will see that the danger is daily becoming more imminent:

"On yesterday 3,000 rebels, west of Bird's Point 40 miles; 300 at Madrid, and three regiments from Union City ordered there; also troops from Randolph and Corinth. *The number of organized rebels within fifty miles of me will exceed twelve thousand*—that is including Randolph troops ordered and not including several companies opposite in Kentucky."

Again, on the 1st day of August, he telegraphed General Fremont a still darker prospect, as follows. (New Madrid is on the Mississippi river, south of Cairo, and not very distant:)

"The following information just received is, I believe, very reliable. *General Pillow was at New Madrid on the morning of the 31st, with eleven thousand troops well armed and well drilled; two regiments of cavalry splendidly equipped; one battery of flying artillery, ten pounders, an i ten guns manned and officered by foreigners; several mountain howitzers and other artillery, amounting in all to one hundred. Nine thousand more moving to reinforce.* He has promised Governor Jackson to place twenty thousand men in Missouri at once. I have a copy of his proclamation and also one of his written passes."

These dispatches came pouring in upon General Fremont from this exposed and important position, vital not only for Illinois but for the whole Union, where there were but eight regiments, only two of which they had a right to hold there, the remaining six being three months' men whose term had expired, and the rebels were forming round them twenty thou sand strong. McClellan, but ten days before, had, in reply to Lyon's appeals, in the telegram I have quoted, expressly pointed to Cairo as a threatened position, and had alluded to the inadequate forces at his command even for *its* defence. What should an officer do under such circumstances? "Fremont did the best he could; he got together all the men he could, and went down with steamboats to Cairo. And for this he was condemned all over the country, because he went down there with steamboats and "made a parade," when really it was useful, because it impressed the secessionists and capitalists of St. Louis with the conviction that he had a larger force than he really had. But let me say, in passing, just here, that great complaint was made because General Fremont went down to the boat in a carriage and four. My friend did not speak of it, but the charge has been in circulation all over the country. Now, the facts in relation to that matter are just these, as I learned at St. Louis. His friends, without his knowledge, when the expedition was ready to start, brought a carriage and four to his house for him to ride down to the boat in. When Fremont came to the door, and saw it, he positively refused to ride in it, preferring to walk to the levee or to go in an ordinary carriage. But his friends told him that it had been said that he dare not show himself to the people for fear of being assassinated, and it was necessary that he should go down to the boat as publicly as possible, in order to show that there was no truth in the report; and thereupon Fremont consented to enter the carriage, and this was added to the charges against him.

I have heard a great deal, too—and the House will pardon me for these digressions, as a few incidental points strike my mind while speaking—about a costly $6,000 house which he hired in St. Louis for himself and his staff. I have been in that house, and so has my friend from St. Louis; for at one time both he and I were able to pass its "barricades." Other generals and other officers have found that they must exclude most of the thousand visitors desiring to see them. if they wished to attend to their grave and responsible trusts; but from one end of the country to the other Fre-

mont was denounced for these barricades. I found out this in regard to that celebrated house : that the officers crowded into that one house, where they were at the instant call of the commanding general, no time lost in sending messengers from one office to another, but all under the same roof, and the telegraph with them, would, if they had been in seperate quarters, have been allowed, under the Army regulations, $6 400 for quarters. Fremont paid $6,000 a year for this house, and yet he has been denounced for that as an evidence of his reckless extravagance.

There is another thing to which I wish to refer before I leave these minor points. When I reached St. Louis at one time, I heard a great many sneers about Fremont having ordered five hundred tons of ice, and about the glorious time he and his staff would have with their sherry cobblers, &c., on their march to southwest Missouri. I made inquiry about it, and found that it was on a requisition from the surgeon that this ice was supplied. It was not to accompany the army, but to be used in the hospitals along the railroads, where the sick were suffering, and to which the wounded, after battle, would, if possible, have been brought. It made my heart bleed to think that the General commanding should be denounced for this. In some of the Indiana regiments, my own fellow-citizens, for whose sufferings in the field and the hospital I have felt deeply, nearly half the men were lying sick from fevers contracted by malaria and exposure, and because they were not used to the muddy water of the Missouri. After they went into hospital, and drank the same water, they continued sick. One regiment, the twenty-second, had a majority in hospital from the malaria and the drinking of this water. The surgeons asked for ice for hospital purposes, for the sick and suffering men who had gone out to fight, to suffer, and to die, if needs be, for their country. And for yielding to that, and showing, as he always has, a deep solicitude for the men under his command, Fremont was denounced in St. Louis and all over the country. Let the denunciation go on. The brave men whose parched lips were thus cooled will not forget the man who has been thus condemned for this additional act of "extravagance."

But, Mr. Chairman, I have no time to examine and explain all the charges—"thick as the leaves in Vallambrosa"—which have been made against him. The balance, or most of them, at least, are of a piece with those to which I have alluded. Let them all pass.

THE SADDEST DAYS IN MISSOURI.

My friend says that the "hundred days" of Fremont were the saddest days for all the loyal persons in Missouri that they had seen. I differ with him in that. There was a sadder day for them than those. It was after Fremont was deposed, and after this army that had gone forth with banners and music to south-western Missouri, and the enemy fleeing before them, took up its line of merch back to the line of the railroad, and the more densely populated settlements. The people of southwestern Missouri, who, in the exuberance of their zeal, when they saw the Stars and Stripes borne by Fremont's army, had clapped their hands with joy, and proclaimed themselves for the Union—these men, from the very heights of confidence and hope, were plunged into the very valley of despondency by this forward movement being changed into a retreat. And when the army took up its backward march, they, knowing what fate they might expect to meet from the vengeance of the rebel hordes of Price—the halter, the prison, outrage and robbery, tyranny and spoliation—followed that army, with their sorrowing families, in sad procession, back to St. Louis, penniless and homeless, when, had Fremont not been superseded, the army would have gone on with the banner they had welcomed full high advanced, instead of coming back and leaving all southwest Missouri to be ravaged by traitors, until three months afterwards a more fortunate general led another army over the same route that Fremont had trodden, and on the same mission. No, sir ; *that* was the saddest day that the loyal men of Missouri had ever seen.

FREMONT'S PROCLAMATION.

My friend has said that the proclamation of General Fremont was bombastic. I cannot turn aside from this argument to analyze its sentences and to discuss the question whether it was bombastic or firm and decided ; whether it was a mere flourish of the pen, or intended to prove that those who embarked in rebellion should find it a costly experiment, not only as to their lives, but also as to their possessions. The President modified it, as he had a constitutional right to do. I have never quarreled with the President because he saw fit to say that that proclamation must be changed. I regret that he was of that opinion. But I know Mr. Lincoln to be an honest mau—as honest and as conscientious and true-hearted a man as walks the earth ; and I know he must have taken this position because he felt, looking over the whole country, that that seemed to be his duty. Whether he erred or Fremont erred, I would be the last man to asperse any of Mr. Lincoln's acts, when they are based, as all know they are, on his convictions. When the President ordered the proclamation to be modified, General Fremont replied in a letter, moderate and not "bombastic," wherein he says he prefers, if the President feels it necessary, he should himself modify it ; and that he would bow to the order, as a subordinate should always bow to the rebuke of his chief. The following was his reply to the President's dissent from his proclamation :

"Trusting to have your confidence, I have been leaving it to events themselves to show you whether or not I was shaping affairs here according to your ideas The shortest communication between Washington and St. Louis generally involves two days, and the employment of two days in time of war goes largely toward success or disaster. I, therefore, went along according to my own Judgment, leaving the result of my movements to Justify me with you And so in regard to my proclamation of August 30th. Between the rebel armies, the Provisional Government, and home traitors, I felt the position bad, and saw danger. In the night I decided upon the proclamation, and the form of it. I wrote it the next morning and printed it the same day. I did it without consultation or advice with any one, acting solely with my best Judgment to serve the country and yourself, and perfectly willing to receive the amount of censure which should be thought due if I made a false movement This is as much a movement in the war as a battle; and in going into these I shall have to act according to my judgment of the ground before me, as I did on this occasion If, upon reflection, your better Judgment still decides that I am wrong in the article respecting the liberation of slaves, I have to ask that you will openly direct me to make the correction. The implied censure will be received as a soldier always should the reprimand of his chief. If I were to retract of my own accord it would imply that I myself thought it wrong, and that I had acted without the reflection which the gravity of the point demanded. But I did not. I acted with full deliberation. and upon the certain conviction that it was a measure right and necessary ; and I think so still."

I think my friend might have spared the sarcastic remarks which he made about the threatened mutiny at Springfield when General Fremont was removed from command. I have the assurance of a gentleman from Indiana, whose word is as good as my oath, or any other man's oath—I mean Col. Hudson, the agent of the State of Ind ana—who was there at the time, that there was sadness all over the camp when the news came that Fremont was actually superseded. This may have been unjust to his successor. It may have been unwarranted ; but still the fact was so. The fact also exists that Fremont's utmost influence was promptly exerted to preserve subordination among his troops. He bowed, without a murmur, to the decision, though it took from him the coveted opportunity of vindicating himself against all who had attacked him, and he demanded that all under his command should cordially obey his successor. His farewell to the "Mississippi army"—which he had labored so earnestly. against all adverse circumstances, to organize ; which he had led, by forced marches that seem incredible, almost into the presence of the retreating enemy, and which was the only army of the Union that had, up to that time, been led fifty miles away from a railroad or a navigable water-course—has been read, not only in our own but also in foreign lands, even by men who, with the multiplied charges against him, had doubted his capacity, with moistened eyes, as they saw how nobly that man, thus stricken down, fell without a word of complaint, and closed his military career in the western deparment by stirring words of encouragement to the gallant soldiers from whom he was thus separated. Even one of the leading New York papers that denounced him spoke in highly eulogistic language of the manner in which he met his fate.* And

* Headquarters Western Department,
Springfield, Mo., Nov. 2, 1861.
Soldiers of the Mississippi Army : Agreeably to orders this

when twenty thousand of the constituents of my friend from Ohio, [Mr. GURLEY,] who had been on his staff, came thronging to honor the fallen General, and offered him an ovation in the city of Cincinnati, he declined it, and passed through without accepting any hospitality. Six months have passed since then. Has there been a man who bore himself so meekly? He visits New York, after official consent was at last obtained for him to leave St. Louis, and refuses the complimentary reception that thousands would gladly have joined in. No word of bitterness or complaint falls from his lips. He comes to this city, subpoenaed by a congressional committee, to testify as to his management of his responsible trust. He comes here, and bears himself as modestly as in New York. Do you see any parade of his gaping wounds to the people? Not at all. He has not even prompted me to say a single word in his behalf, although he knows me to be his friend. I have not asked him for a single fact in reference to his case, because I wanted to speak independently here, as a Representative of the people. He doubtless longs to be in the service of his country at this hour of her peril. And though he may chafe at inaction, as his heart bounds at the thought of being again at the head of advancing squadrons driving the enemies of the country before him, have you seen a single line of complaint from his pen against those who counseled his supersedure?

But, to recur to his proclamation. Let me ask what difference was there in substance between that proclamation and the celebrated remark in Cincinnati of ANDREW JOHNSON, that loyal, Jacksonlike and heroic Senator from Tennessee, whom all true men in the country cherish in their heart of hearts? He said, about the very time when Fremont issued his proclamation, "that no rebel had a right to own anything." Fremont said that the real and personal property of rebels should be confiscated to the public use, and that their slaves, if they had any, should be declared free men; and ANDREW JOHNSON, a slaveholding Senator from a slaveholding State, said that no rebel had a right to own anything. I can see no difference between the two, except that Fremont,

day received, I take leave of you. Our army has been of sudden growth, and we have grown up together, and I have become familiar with the brave and generous spirits which you bring to the defence of your country, and which makes me anticipate for you a brilliant career.

Continue as you have begun, and give to my successor the same cordial and enthusiastic support with which you have encouraged me. Emulate the splendid example which you have already before you, and let me remain, as I am, proud of the noble army which I have thus far labored to bring together.

Soldiers, I regret to leave you most sincerely. I thank you for the regard and confidence you have invariably shown to me. I deeply regret that I shall not have the honor to lead you to the victory which you are just about to win; but I shall claim to share with you in the joy of every triumph, and trust always to be fraternally remembered by my companions in arms.

JOHN C. FREMONT,
Major General U. S. A.

as a commanding general, desiring thus to weaken the power and cripple the resources of the traitors, embodied it in a proclamation, as the Senator did in a sentence.

THE FALL OF LEXINGTON.

I come now to the siege and fall of Lexington. I think I have shown, by General Lyon's own statement, that he did not arraign Fremont for not being strengthened and succored; and I should have added then that Fremont arrived in St. Louis only fourteen days before Lyon's death. I have shown where General Lyon thought the responsibility rested. I have shown the dispatch from General McClellan, only six days before Fremont arrived at St. Louis, saying that there were only enough troops and arms to reinforce Cairo, and that the troops he could spare, and but two regiments at that, must *only* be used to defend St. Louis, and only then "in case of absolute necessity." I will now leave that part of the subject and come to the surrender of Mulligan at Lexington. I think I can make out as strong a vindication for General Fremont there. I am glad to see that my friend from Missouri is paying so much attention. The attachment between him and me has been such, that it is the most painful duty of my life to have to differ from him to-day on such a subject. I would far rather meet any one else here in the collision of conflicting views; but we can differ, I know, as friends should differ when their roads separate.

My friend said that troops could be got in every direction to defend Cairo. Now here is a dispatch from Governor Morton, of Indiana, in response to Fremont's pressing appeal, dated the 4th of August, three days after Fremont went to Cairo, and six days before Lyon was killed:

"Can send five regiments if leave is granted by the Department, *as I am ordered to send them East* as fast as ready."

Now, to show also how General Fremont was "aided" at that time, here is a dispatch from Washington, eight days before Lyon died, and when Cairo, from General Prentiss's dispatches, was so bare of artillery:

WASHINGTON, *August* 2, 1861.

To Major Gen. J. C. FREMONT, Cairo:

This dispatch was sent yesterday to commanding officer department, Ohio, Cincinnati. Order two (2) companies fourth artillery, with their batteries, under Howard and Kingsbury, to St. Louis without delay.

WINFIELD SCOTT.
M. BLAIR, *P. M. G.*

I doubt not Fremont's heart bounded as he read of this timely aid coming to his relief.

But here is another dispatch from General Scott *of the same day:*

WAR DEPARTMENT,
Washington, August 2, 1861.

To General FREMONT:

Since ordering the two batteries for you yesterday, it appears one company has no guns and the other is in Western Virginia; neither can be withdrawn. *The order is countermanded.*

WINFIELD SCOTT.

I will not comment on the disappointment the General must have felt; but he toiled on with almost daily drawbacks like these. .

I come now to Lexington. I happened on the 14th of September to be in the city of St. Louis, when the whole city was excited at the news which had just reached it that Price was marching on that gallant and devoted band at Lexington; and when my friend spoke about the home guards which General Fremont had under him, it reminded me that Colonel Mulligan did not bear testimony to the efficiency of the home guards at Lexington.

Mr. BLAIR, of Missouri. If Colonel Mulligan made such a statement, he is not as magnanimous as he is brave. I will undertake to prove that the home guards in the trenches at Lexington bore themselves as gallantly as did Colonel Mulligan, or any other man who was there. Colonel Grover was wounded, and died of his wounds; Colonel Peabody was badly wounded; Colonel White is still disabled by wounds received in that fight; and the gallant major of the Kansas City home guards, whose name at this moment, I am ashamed to say, has slipped my memory, also received honorable wounds. Thus it will be seen that the commanding officer of every battalion of home guards was wounded; and as large a proportion of men were killed and wounded as among the Illinois regiments. No man should disparage those who have shed their blood for the country.

Mr. COLFAX. Colonel Mulligan's testimony is the reverse of that. I was not there, and therefore do not know.

Mr. BLAIR, of Missouri. These are the facts of the case.

Mr. COLFAX. I wish my friend to understand that I do not arraign the home guards at all. I do not arraign anybody. I am simply on the defence, and am stating the facts from history, and from official documents, which can be read by the whole country. I only made the passing remark that Mulligan did not regard the home guards as valuable auxiliaries in his defence, though my friend cites their number in various towns as part of Fremont's *effective* force.

When I arrived at St. Louis on the 14th of September I saw Lieutenant Governor Hall. He told me that Price was marching through the centre of Missouri, up toward Lexington, with fifteen thousand men, and that Fremont ought to send out a column for the purpose of intercepting and capturing them. I asked him how many men Fremont had in St. Louis. He said he had twenty thousand men, and spoke with great positiveness as to the number. I thought if that was correct there was no excuse for not sending them, and went to headquarters at once to see General Fremont. I told him it was represented that he had twenty thousand men at St. Louis, that Price was marching on Lexington with a large

force, and urged that a force be sent without delay to cut him off. He replied: "Mr. COLFAX, I will tell you, confidentially, how many men we have in St. Louis, though I would not have it published on the streets for my life. The opinion in the city is that we have twenty thousand men here, and this gives us strength. If it were known where what was the actual number, our enemies would be promptly informed. But I will show you how many there are." He rang the bell, and his secretary brought in the muster-rolls of the morning. I read them, and there were in the city and for a circuit of seven miles round, less than eight thousand men, home guards and all. There were actually but two full regiments, and the remainder of the force was made up of fragmentary and undisciplined regiments of two hundred and fifty, four hundred, and six hundred men. It was a beggarly array of an army in proportion to what was needed at that time for the defence even of that city against enemies without or within, and I told him so. "But," said I, "can't you spare some of these men?" The tears stood in his eyes as he handed me two telegraphic dispatches, just received by him, which I read then with pain and sadness, and will read now, and the House can judge how they aided him in his plans for the reinforcement of Mulligan, or the capture of Price's army:

WASHINGTON, *September* 14, 1861.
To Major General FREMONT:
On consultation with the President and head of Department, it was determined to call upon you for five thousand well-armed infantry, to be sent here without a moment's delay. Give them three days cooked rations. This draft from your forces to be replaced by you from the States of Illinois, Iowa, Kansas, &c. How many men have you under arms in your district? Please answer fully and immediately   SIMON CAMERON,
Secretary of War.

WASHINGTON, *September* 14, 1861.
To Major General FREMONT:
Detach five thousand infantry from your department to come here without delay, and report the number of the troops that will be left with you. The President dictates.
WINFIELD SCOTT.

I have shown you before that there were regiments there waiting, without guns, and yet, when, under these desperate circumstances, General Fremont bought guns, the best he could get, he was denounced because they were not Springfield muskets or Enfield rifles, or the best arms known to the service. He was not allowed to send unarmed regiments, to be armed after they reached Washington, or on the road. From these he could have filled the order easily. But they must be "well-armed infantry." And he had been begging for "arms, arms of any kind," the whole fifty days he had then been in command in the West, but mostly in vain. And now, "five thousand well-armed infantry" were needed, "without a moment's delay," to swell the forces of the army of the Potomac. I do not allude to this to criticise. Like Fremont, I believe the capital of the country was, first of all, to be defended; but if he was foiled in his plans by demands like these, at such a critical moment, impartial history hereafter will show that it was his misfortune, not his fault.

Mr. BINGHAM. What is the date of those dispatches?

Mr. COLFAX. Saturday, the 14th of September; the very day I was there—just six days before the fall of Lexington—for I wish the House to remember that Mulligan surrendered Friday, September 20. I asked him what he would do, and my heart sank as I asked. Here was the best of his forces ordered away to Washington. I told him I would, if in his place, telegraph to Mr. Lincoln that he had not the eighty thousand efficient soldiers in his department that rumor stated he had; that Missouri would be lost if the troops were taken away. "No," said he, "that would be insubordination, with which I have already been unjustly charged. The capital must be again in danger, and must be saved, even if Missouri fall and I sacrifice myself."

After that interview, after the noble and patriotic sentiment that fell from his lips, I should have been false to my convictions of right and justice, if I had not stood up here to-day and defended the man who was willing, even at his own sacrifice, to save the capital of the nation.

Mr. BLAIR, of Missouri. The gentleman says General Fremont on that day took out the muster-rolls, and showed him how many troops there were at St. Louis.

Mr. COLFAX. Yes, sir; less than eight thousand.

Mr. BLAIR, of Missouri. It so happens that on that same day—the 14th of September—General Fremont returned to Simon Cameron, Secretary of War, the following statement of the forces under his command:

St. Louis, (including home guard).................. 6,890
Under Brigadier General Pope,(including home guard) 5,483
Lexington, (including home guard).................. 2,400
Jefferson City, (one-quarter home guard)........... 9,677
Rolla... 4,700
Trenton.. 3,057
Cape Girardeau................................... 650
Bird's Point and Norfolk.......................... 3,510
Cairo, (including McClernand's brigade)........... 4,826
Fort Holt, opposite Cairo, Kentucky shore.......... 3,595
Paducah.. 7,791
Under General Lane............................... 2,200
Mound City, near Cairo........................... 900

                                                   55,693

Thus you will see that there were some twenty thousand men at and about Cairo; and you will further see, by reference to the documents, that, under the order the gentleman has read, not a man was sent out of Missouri, and but two regiments were started from his department at all. Two regiments, I believe, left his department, and went as far as General Buell's department, and went no further. The order was countermanded, and no more troops sent. The two regiments started were, I believe, Illinois troops in or about Cairo and Paducah. General

Fremont did not send a man out of Missouri, I repeat, under that order, and he was not required to do it. So that the explanation which the gentleman gives, and which General Fremont gives, by way of excusing himself for not sending reinforcements to Colonel Mulligan, about this order to send five thousand men to Washington, amounts to just this: that no troops were sent to Washington at all under that order; only two regiments were sent from his department under it, and none from Missouri under it.

Mr. COLFAX. The gentleman from Missouri occupied two hours in his speech, and he has taken a considerable portion of my time since. I shall only ask to be allowed to go on after the expiration of my hour for the time that has been taken from me; and I do not know that the committee will give me that, [cries of "Oh, yes!"] I presume a majority of the committee will give their consent, but a single member has the power to prevent it.

I will enlighten my friend from Missouri now on the point he has cited. When this order came to send five regiments to Washington, General Fremont sent down to Carondelet and ordered the twenty-fourth Indiana regiment, one of the only two full regiments he had in St. Louis or its vicinity, to proceed to Washington, but the officers of the regiment came up to his headquarters and urged him to allow them to remain in Missouri; and that is the reason they did not go. He then changed the order, and like a faithful subordinate he telegraphed to Washington that he was preparing to obey the order—although it made his heart bleed. Here are the dispatches:

HEADQUARTERS WESTERN DEPARTMENT,
St. Louis, September 14, 1861.
To Colonel E. D. TOWNSEND, A. A. G., Washington City:
I am preparing to obey the orders received this evening for the five regiments.   J. C FREMONT,
Major General Commanding.

HEADQUARTERS WESTERN DEPARTMENT
St. Louis, September 14, 1861.
To General THOMAS, A. G, Washington City:
I am preparing to obey the orders received this evening from the Secretary of War for the five regiments I also send messenger.   J. C. FREMONT,
Major General Commanding.

True, as the gentleman from Missouri says, the order was at last partially countermanded; but, when days were almost years, he was engaged in preparations for sending on three more regiments of "well-armed infantry," besides the two he did send, for FOUR DAYS out of the six that elapsed between the order from Washington and the fall of Lexington; and engaged besides in the most vigorous attempts, out of his scattered forces in the vast area of disloyal territory they were holding, from Paducah to the Kansas frontier, to reinforce the imperilled Mulligan. Here is the countermanding order, after four days and nights of anxious labors to comply both with duty on one side and orders on the other, for which his reward has been a sad one indeed:

WASHINGTON, *September* 18, 1861.
To Major Gen. FREMONT :

General Scott acquiesces to your wishes in your proposition to retain troops not already forwarded. He has telegraphed order to retain the two regiments which have left for Cincinnati to wait orders for a few days; if they have not passed beyond that city.

E. D. TOWNSEND.

Let us return to Mulligan's peril. Thinking there might still be hope of obtaining reinforcements by appealing to the Governors of States near at hand, for, if they could send troops immediately to St. Louis, he could order up all his available forces there by steamboat toward Lexington, he telegraphed, on this very 14th of September, to Governor Morton and Governor Dennison, of Indiana and Ohio, for help. And these are the replies, (Mr. Coggeshall was Governor Dennison's military secretary :)

INDIANAPOLIS, *September* 14, 1861.

We have received *orders to send all available forces to Washington.*

O. P. MORTON, *Governor of Indiana.*

COLUMBUS, OHIO, *September* 15, 1861.

No troops are ordered to ʰastern Virginia. *All our troops are ordered to Western Virginia.* Dennison is in Washington.

W. T. COGGESHALL.

His only remaining hope was in his own men, his scattered forces, to weaken himself at some points on his long line to save Lexington, if possible. And what did he do? My friend says—and I have his exact words—"it cannot be shown that he moved one single man towards Lexington at all." Lexington fell on Friday, the 20th of September. I shall remember the day to the last hour of my life; for I watched, as did my constituents, day by day and hour by hour for news from there, with a solicitude that excluded all thought of all other questions.

General Fremont telegraphed in every direction. He ordered General Pope to come down to Lexington and reinforce Mulligan there; he ordered General Sturgis to come down and reinforce him; he ordered Jefferson C. Davis, of Indiana, acting brigadier general at Jefferson City, to go forward and reinforce him. He used every means in his power. The telegraphic wires were hot with his dispatches, sent in every direction, to secure the reinforcement of Mulligan. See the columns of them of these eventful days in the official dispatches, at last published in the New York *Tribune*, and which attest his sleepless energy so strikingly. Now, four days before Mulligan surrendered, see what General Pope telegraphs:

PALMYRA, *September* 16, 1861.

To Major General FREMONT :

From paper just handed me, I learn, *for the first time,* that important matters are occurring at Lexington. *The troops I sent to Lexington will be there the day after to-morrow, and consist of two full regiments of infantry, four pieces of artillery, and* 150 *irregular horse. These, with the two Ohio regiments, which will reach there on Thursday, will make a reinforcement of* 4,000 *men and four pieces of artillery.* Do you wish me to come down to St. Louis, or go to Canton and Keokuk to finish matters in this section? The following force along this road is Hannibal : At Kansas, 480 ; at Palmyra, 320 of twentieth Illinois ; at Hudson, 420 of Taster's men ; at Brookfield, 650 of Morgan's regiment ; at St Joseph, coming east, 3,000 Iowa and Missouri irregular troops. Please answer to Quincy.

JOHN POPE, *Brigadier General.*

So that General Fremont had the promise, that on the 18th, two days before Lexington actually fell, two full regiments, four cannon, and one hundred and fifty cavalry should succor the brave garrison there holding out, and that by Thursday, the 19th, one day before Mulligan surrendered, the reinforcement from Pope's forces for Lexington should be increased still further, to four thousand men. That they did not arrive there and save it, is not Fremont's fault, then.

Nor was this all. On the 13th of September, the day before I arrived there, it was supposed at St. Louis that Price's advance threatened Booneville; and Fremont telegraphed General Sturgis, then in north Missouri, as follows:

HEADQUARTERS WESTERN DEPARTMENT,
St. Louis, September 13, 1861.

SIR : Information having been received at these headquarters of an intended attack on Booneville, you are hereby ordered to move at once by the shortest possible route, and with all practicable speed, direct to that place with your force of infantry and artillery.

J. C. FREMONT,
Major General Commanding.

To Brigadier General STURGIS, *Mexico.*

But on the eventful 14th of September it was discovered that the attack would probably be on Lexington, and he telegraphed again to Sturgis, as follows :

HEADQUARTERS WESTERN DEPARTMENT,
St. Louis, September 14, 1861.

SIR : You are hereby directed to move, via Utica, with all practicable speed, to Lexington, on the Missouri river, with your force of infantry and artillery. You will send back the three companies of the Fremont hussars, under Captain Blum, to St. Louis.

The most practicable route from Utica to Lexington for you will be by Austinville, Finneys' Grove, and Morton.

J. C. FREMONT,
Major General Commanding.

To Brigadier General STURGIS, *Mexico.*

On the 13th, he twice telegraphs to Acting Brigadier General Jeff. C. Davis, at Jefferson City, to send forward two regiments to strengthen Lexington, and says, "move promptly." On the 14th he telegraphs him that he is sending him up regiments and batteries from St. Louis, while he also notifies the Department at Washington that they should have the five regiments they demanded from him—two from St. Louis, two from Cairo and vicinity, and one from Illinois—absolutely stripping himself in St Louis of every means of defence to comply with these wants in every direction. Not content with issuing orders, you find nearly half a dozen the same day to the same officer, urging celerity, energy, rapid movement. No man living could have done more. I add here the official dispatch to Jeff. C. Davis :

HEADQUARTERS WESTERN DEPARTMENT,
St. Louis, September 14, 1861.

SIR : As a column of the enemy's force is moving upon Lexington, you are hereby directed immediately to order two of the regiments under your command to the reinforcement of that place. Orders have already been issued to two regiments in this city to proceed to Jefferson City, and reinforce your command.

Brigadier General Sturgis, now at Mexico, will also repair to Lexington with his entire force of infantry and a battery of artillery. ·On his arrival, he will assume command of all troops at that place.

J. C. FREMONT,
Major General Commanding.

˙ To Colonel JEFF. C. DAVIS,
Colonel Commanding at Jefferson City.

Now, let us examine what was done. Pope's reinforcements did not arrive ; General Sturgis did come to a point near the river on the opposite side from Lexington; and I have the testimony of Colonel `Mulligan himself that if he had ac ually come within sight with his forces on the opposite side of the river, Price had got so tired of fighting, the defence had been so persistent and unyielding, that he would have retired, notwithstanding his force of twenty thousand men, with eight brigadier generals, besieging one colonel of the Union forces. But the evidence is, that Sturgis came down to a point within a few miles of the river, and learning that the ferry-boats had , been destroyed, and that, therefore, it was impossible for him to cross the river, and learning from a contraband—for they were permitted then to come within our lines and give information as to rebel movements—that Price's force was twenty to twenty-five thousand, deeming that he had not a force sufficient to meet them, as he had not, he retired. Fremont, however, supposed that, by four days after his order to him, he would have reached Lexington; and on the 18th—two days before Lexington fell—he sent orders to him at that point.

Jefferson C. Davis, upon the reception of General Fremont's orders, embarked as soon as possible—for it takes time—his available force upon some steamboats; and they proceeded up the river to a place called Glasgow, where, learning that the rebels had erected batteries, they landed for the purpose of storming them before proceeding under their fire ; ·and in the darkness of the night they fired into each other, and being thrown into confusion, they did not get to Lexington in time to reinforce Colonel Mulligan.

These three forces from different directions, then, set out under the orders of General Fremont to reinforce the gallant defenders of Lexington, and he failed in accomplishing that purpose because the elements seemed to be against him, and not because he did not seek in every possible way to succor that besieged garrison. His dispatches to his secret agents are not, of course, published; but a reply from one of them, Charles Noyes, says that Sturgis was expected to reach Lexington the Wednesday night before the surrender, and General Lane the Thursday night before. Fate seemed to prevent these reinforcements, not the inactivity or indifference of Fremont.

Now, to appreciate the difficulties General Fremont had to contend with in bringing any considerable number of men to any one point, you must remember the extended frontier, and the large number of posts he had to defend. Troops were˙stationed, and had to be, not only at St. Louis and Cairo, but all through north Missouri, at Lexington, at Jefferson City, at Rolla, at Ironton, at Cape Girardeau, at Bird's Point, at Fort Holt, opposite Cairo, at Norfolk, at Mound City, at Paducah, and many other points. Judge Blair testifies how difficult it was for him, here, at the capital, and with the influence wielded by a member of the Cabinet, to obtain any attention to Western interests, or compliance with Western requisitions. But Fremont, with troops constantly ordered away from him, with a plentiful lack of guns, with credit impaired, if not ruined, by the possibility of his removal, (and since then these creditors have seen their claims delayed for months, till examined by a board of commissioners, and even still unpaid,) was expected to organize victory, and triumph over every adverse circumstance.

But let us look further, and see what was the condition of affairs' when Price marched upon Lexington. Why, sir, at the very time when Price, with from fifteen to twenty thousand men, was threatening Lexington, McCulloch was threatening Rolla and Jefferson City, Hardee was threatening Ironton, in southeast Missouri, and Polk and Pillow, with a number of troops, estimated at twenty to twenty-six thousand, were down at Columbus, threatening our inferior forces at Cairo ; and in addition to that, there were the forces of Jeff. Thompson, Martin Green, and other guerrilla bands ; and there were organized bands of rebels in every county in the State. The State was heaving and seething with insurrection under his feet, and he had to restore it to its loyalty. All this Fremont had to encounter, with nearly eighty thousand rebels threatening all these exposed points, with the disloyalists at their homes, and with an inadequate force to meet the enemy. Sir, a responsibility was thrown upon him which I would not to-day take upon my shoulders for the best office in the gift of the American people or of the world.

THE INVESTIGATING COMMITTEE.

While he was struggling nobly to perform his duty, from every side came the poisoned arrows of calumny, and the *ex parte* testimony of the investigating committee of this House, charging him with connivance with contractors to plunder the Treasury. I regret to have to allude to their course, ˙for every member of the committee, I believe and hope, is my personal friend.

Sir, I have learned to look with some distrust upon *ex parte* testimony. I recollect that when my friend from Ohio, [Mr. SHERMAN,] who now occupies a seat at the other end of the Capitol, was at the head of a committee sitting in judgment upon the then Secretary of the Navy, Mr. Toucey, they wrote to Secretary Toucey, as I found in re-reading their report recently, that they were going to examine into the live oak contract and other matters, and that he would be welcome to come and listen to the evidence; and subsequently, when they had taken the evidence of eight witnesses, they had a correct copy of it made and sent it to Secretary Toucey, with a respectful letter, offering to subpœna any witnesses he might desire to have called; and when subsequent witnesses appeared before them, they took the same course. This was an example of impartiality towards a political opponent worthy of admiration and imitation.

Let me add, also, what is well known to this House, that when the celebrated investigating committee, presided over by my friend from Pennsylvania, [Mr. COVODE,] were engaged in the labor of exposing the corruptions of Mr. Buchanan's administration, their chairman was careful to furnish promptly, not only to the President, but also to his Cabinet ministers, copies of all testimony implicating them, thus giving them an opportunity of knowing what was charged against them, of disproving the charges if incorrect, or of explaining them away if they were susceptible of explanation.

But how was it in the case of Fremont? I undertake to say, and history proves it, that while Fremont was out hunting the enemy, some persons—not the committee, perhaps, but his enemies in St. Louis—were hunting up witnesses against him to have *ex parte* testimony taken there; and no sooner was it taken, while he was still in the face of the foe endeavoring to obtain victory for our arms and periling his life for his country, a synopsis of these *ex parte* statements was given by some one to some newspaper correspondent, and sent upon the wires all over the country, so as to poison the public mind against the commander of the department of the West, and assist in achieving his overthrow. Sir, I think that in common justice, in common humanity—if there are such things as justice and humanity—when he returned, a deposed general, the committee might, if they did not see fit to do so before, have sent him the adverse evidence, which up to this hour they have never done, and said to him: "Sir, before you were sent to this department you were supposed to be an honest man, but this testimony clouds your character. It was taken in your absence; if you have any vindication or defence to offer, we will subpœna your witnesses, and give their testimony to the world in company with that taken against you while you were in the field." But no; the testimony was never sent to him, and he has never seen it, unless some member of the House ere this has lent him a copy; he has had no official information concerning it.

My friend from Missouri says that Fremont has not demanded a trial. I wish to ask him if he did not make charges against General Fremont before the late Secretary of War, Mr. Cameron?

Mr. BLAIR, of Missouri. Certainly.

Mr. COLFAX. Then I wish to say this: that if Secretary Cameron, the Minister of War, thought those charges worthy of consideration, it was *his* duty to have put Fremont on trial. I wish to ask my friend now, if he has not also made charges against General Fremont before the present Secretary of War?

Mr. BLAIR, of Missouri. I preferred charges against him at the time, and the gentleman knows very well that I have preferred no charges since; but I know that the Judge Advocate has preferred charges since.

Mr. COLFAX. Then, if the present Secretary of War deems them worthy of investigation, it is his duty to order a trial. General Fremont has the same right as the meanest and wickedest man in the country has—the right to meet his accusers face to face, and to stand up in his own defence, and vindicate himself against these charges.

My friend was arrested by General Fremont, and I feel authorized to say that I went to Fremont at the time and remonstrated with him, and spoke in terms of condemnation of his arrest of my friend as being unwise and wrong; that the country would regard it as the result of a personal quarrel, &c. Sincerely the friend of both, I desired, if possible, to restore friendly relations between them. It was during the dark days of which I have spoken; but General Fremont replied that it was for insubordination; that he could not expect subordination in others, if, on account of my friend's influence and power, which he did not underrate, he passed his by in silence. Still, I deeply regretted it. But when my friend was discharged by order of General Scott, did he think it necessary for his character that, after having been thus discharged, he should still insist on a trial?

Mr. BLAIR, of Missouri. Yes, sir; and I did demand a trial.

Mr. COLFAX. But none was had. Then, if my friend has made charges against General Fremont, and the War Department, either under Mr. Cameron or Mr. Stanton, deemed the charges such as substantially affect his present rank, it was their duty to arraign him and put him on trial.

Mr. BLAIR, of Missouri. Charges have been preferred against him by the proper officer of the Government—the judge advocate of the United States.

Mr. WADSWORTH asked a question in reference to the contract for the fortifications of St. Louis, which was inaudible at the reporters' desk.

Mr. COLFAX. I am speaking now, not on dollars and cents, but to vindicate the history of the past; but I will answer the gentleman from Kentucky as follows: I said at the opening of my remarks, if the gentleman had been kind enough to listen to me, which I suppose he did not, that I did not defend the fortification contract, nor did I deem it wise or economical.

Mr. WADSWORTH. I heard the gentleman say so.

Mr. COLFAX. I am not called upon to defend that contract, but in justice to General Fremont, it ought to be stated that the contractor offered, if the work could be done by day only, instead of day and night uninterruptedly, when he would have to pay extra for night work, to do it for sixty per cent. less; but Fremont said, "time is worth more than money; do the work immediately, with all the force you can put on, working night and day"—for he was just then preparing for his march against Price. He needed all available troops, and, with the fortifications, he could leave St. Louis with a smaller force for its defence.

But I want now to put a question to the gentleman, *argumentum ad hominum*, as he has opened this question. Suppose you find that some claim has passed this Congress which everybody concedes to be entirely wrong and inexcusable; and suppose some man looking over the Globe finds, on the list of yeas and nays on the vote by which that money was improperly taken out of the Treasury, that Mr. WADSWORTH voted for it, and arraigns him before the people for it. This, on *ex parte* evidence, would look badly. Here is a cheating claim on the Treasury, the people would say, and the claimant gets his money out of our Treasury by the direct aid and consent of our Representative's vote. But there are two sides to it. The gentleman from Kentucky rises and says, "Does not my defamer know that the Committee of Claims reported favorably upon that claim, and that it is the custom of members of Congress to follow the report of the Committee of Claims, in cases which they have closely scrutinized, and against which they themselves see no objection?" And when the gentleman has thus been heard in his defence, everybody says that, although he voted for the claim, he is acquitted, because his explanation is satisfactory. That is the only fair way to try a man. Strike, but hear before you strike. If Fremont shall prove that he made this contract to carry on the work day and night until its completion, upon the advice of engineers and men experienced in work of this kind, it will be at least some palliation of it, just as the gentleman's vote in favor of a bad claim, on the recommendation of the proper committee, would palliate it. I do not know what General Fremont's defence is. I have not asked what his defence is.

Mr. WADSWORTH. The case which the gentleman puts is not at all like this case. It appears that Fremont made a contract with an adventurer of the name of Beard for earth works and embankments, at $2 50 per cubic yard for removing the earth, when the committee tell us it was only worth sixty cents a cubic yard—a difference of $1 90.

Now, if I did anything of that sort as a member of Congress, I should say that I was unworthy of holding my seat here, and my constituents would be justified in denouncing my action as the result of bribery or other improper influence.

Mr. COLFAX. I am reminded by a friend near me that General Fremont, in his letter to Senator WADE, the chairman of the committee on the conduct of the war, explains this matter himself. As I do not defend these contracts, deeming them too costly, though I may err against him in that, I will let him make the explanation in his own language.

Mr. WADSWORTH. I have never seen that explanation.

Mr. COLFAX. I am going to read it to you:

"When the prices for his work were under discussion and were referred to me by General McKinstry, I directed this officer to reduce them to what was just and reasonable to both parties, having reference to the circumstances under which the work was done, and the extra prices that had been paid, so as to leave the contractor what might be strictly a fair profit on his labor, and his decision, whatever it was, was approved by me. For cost of construction and other details with which I am not acquainted, I respectfully refer the committee to the testimony of the quartermaster and the contractor, whom I have asked to have summoned.

"To show their nature and value, the report and testimony of the engineers, who planned and who were superintending the work, will be furnished the committee. The object aimed at was the completion of the city defences in the shortest possible time. The works are thoroughly and well built, covering and comprehending the city itself and the surrounding country on a length of about ten miles, and the total cost is, I think, less than $300,000.

"In my judgment, having in view the time and manner in which they were built, the money was well applied, and as a measure of expediency and policy, it was fully worth to the Government what it cost."

This is just exactly what General McClellan and the Secretary of War do every day in the matter of ordnance, and a thousand other things. If Mr. Stanton attends to the business of his department, he would not have time to look after the details of all the contracts that are made for the vast service of that department. He regards the heads of bureaus as his legal advisers in the matter. General Fremont did the same thing with the heads of his— the engineer department, quartermaster, &c., &c. All over the country General Fremont has been held responsible for what General McKinstry had done. He never appointed General McKinstry, nor could he remove him. McKinstry was appointed by the last Administration, and continued at that post by the present one. He was quartermaster general of that post, just as General Meigs is Quartermaster General of the United States. He therefore had the authority to do this thing.

Mr. STEVENS. I understand that McKinstry is a good officer, and was appointed on recommendations of an influential firm doing business partly in this city and partly in St. Louis.

Mr. COLFAX. As I said before, Mr Chairman, I have not attempted to arraign anybody. I have not arraigned the commanding general of the army of the Potomac, or any Cabinet officer, or the President, or anybody else. I have only gathered together the facts of history, collected these official documents that every one can read, and laid them before the House; and with a few remarks in conclusion, I will relieve my fellow-members from listening to me further. ,

The CHAIRMAN. The gentleman has had consent to proceed without limitation as to time.

Mr. COLFAX. I will not take advantage of the good nature of the House. When Fremont was superseded, what was the condition of affairs in Missouri? It has gone into history, and will live there during all time, his proudest and noblest vindication. The whole State, thanks to his energy, was more tranquil on that day than was Western Virginia or Kentucky at that period—all except a little corner down by Arkansas, and an United States officer in uniform could ride alone from Springfield, near the Arkansas line, to St. Louis, unmolested and unharmed; that was certainly one thing not to his discredit.

In the second place, the army which he was heading was further South than any other army of the Union on that day. That was another good sign.

In the third place, it was headed in the right direction—southward, after the enemy. That was still another good sign. He may be a very incompetent general, as my friend insists, though I differ widely from him on that point; but it took three months after his supersedure to get things back to just the point where he left them, saying nothing of all the rebel outrages during the interim.

In the fourth place, the men under his command were filled with loyalty and enthusiasm for him. If he had been this imbecile, this corrupt man, this timid man, this incompetent general, they would have scorned and despised him, and would have revolted against him. The brave life guard commanded by Zagonyi—who, my friend says, won no victory at Springfield—performed the most brilliant achievement of the war up to that time, and lighted up the horizon, after long months of inaction and reverse, with the glorious illumination of that act—the presage of future triumphs for our arms. But that charge upon the enemy, with the war cry of "Fremont and the Union," cost them dearly. When the life guard came back to St. Louis, they were dismissed from service "for words spoken at Springfield." They were refused rations for themselves; they were refused forage for their horses; they were treated with disapproval and almost contempt "for words spoken at Springfield." They were mustered out of service; and Zagonyi, who would gladly give his life to make another such charge on the rebel host,

finds no place open for him in the armies of the Union. They had dared to charge upon the enemy, shouting the name of their chief, whom, perhaps, they

"Loved, not wisely, but *too well*."

But I do insist, however we may differ as to Fremont, that the noble band who hurled themselves on ten times their number, drove them before them by their impetuous charge, and planted the starry banner of the Union on the court-house spire at Springfield, should be spoken of on this floor with admiration of their heroism, and not by endeavoring to underrate their brave endeavor.

In the fifth place, Fremont had marched his army rapidly after the enemy, notwithstanding the adjutant general of the United States, who had seen him on the road, said he could not move it for lack of transportation. Mr. Thurlow Weed, in his letter, which was also thrown in the scale against Fremont, at the trying hour when his supersedure was pending, and he himself was in the field, said the same thing —that Fremont had got to the Osage, but that he could not progress beyond it, and that it was well understood at Warsaw he did not intend to. But, sir, the man who scaled the Rocky Mountains is not the man who stands idle "for lack of transportation." He threw a bridge across the Osage river in thirty-six working hours, infusing into the troops the same energy that has characterized his whole life. The army crossed, and proceeded with forced marches on after the enemy in the right direction. But the moment came that he was to be superseded, and then he fell.

In the sixth place, whatever charges have been made that he unwisely reposed confidence in certain contractors, not even his bitterest enemies have intimated that a single dollar of the people's money, beyond his salary, has stuck to his fingers.

In the seventh and last place, when he left the State of Missouri, all the railroads of the State were running for every mile of their length, and to their full capacity; and he left behind him in the city of St. Louis a monument of his good sense, if not of his genius, in making a connection of all the railroads at the levee, so that the rolling stock of all three could be, in case of a sudden emergency, used on any one of them. That closes his career as the commander of the department of the West; and the duty, of all others, the most grateful to me, vindicating a friend in the hour of trial and adversity, having been performed, it only remains for me to thank the House for the generous extension of time they have given me.

APPENDIX.

Fremont's plan last September for the Kentucky and Tennessee campaign, which was doubtless referred by the President to the General commanding:

[PRIVATE.]

HEADQUARTERS WESTERN DEPARTMENT,
September 8, 1861.

To the PRESIDENT:

MY DEAR SIR: I send by another hand what I ask you to consider in respect to the subject of the note by your special messenger.

In this I desire to ask your attention to the position of affairs in Kentucky. As the rebel troops, driven out from Missouri, had invaded Kentucky in considerable force, and by occupying Union city, Hickman, and Columbus, were preparing to seize Paducah and attack Cairo, I judged it impossible, without losing important advantages, to defer any longer a forward movement. For this purpose I have drawn from the Missouri side a part of the force which had been stationed at Bird's Point, Cairo, and Cape Girardeau, to Fort Holt and Paducah, of which places we have taken possession.* As the rebel forces outnumbered ours, and the counties of Kentucky between the Mississippi and Tennessee rivers, as well as those along the latter and the Cumberland, are strongly secessionist, it becomes imperatively necessary to have the co-operation of the loyal Union forces under Generals Anderson and Nelson, as well as of those already encamped opposite Louisville, under Colonel Rousseau. I have reinforced, yesterday, Paducah with two regiments, and will continue to strengthen the position with men and artillery. As soon as General Smith, who commands there, is reinforced sufficiently for him to spread his forces, he will have to take and hold Mayfield and Lovelaceville, to be in the rear and flank of Columbus, and to occupy Smithland, controlling in this way the mouths of both the Tennessee and the Cumberland rivers. At the same time, Colonel Rousseau should bring his force, increased, if possible, by two Ohio regiments, in boats to Henderson, and, taking the Henderson and Nashville railroad, occupy Hopkinsville, while General Nelson should go with a force of 5,000 by railroad to Louisville, and from there to Bowling Green.*

As the population in all the counties through which the above railroads pass are loyal, this movement could be made without delay or molestation to the troops. Meanwhile, Gen. Grant would take possession of the entire Cairo and Fulton railroad, Piketon, New Madrid, and the shore of the Mississippi opposite Hickman and Columbus.† The foregoing disposition having been effected, a combined attack will be made upon Columbus, and if successful in that, upon Hickman, while Rousseau and Nelson will move in concert, by railroad, to Nashville, Tenn., occupying the State capital, and, with an adequate force, New Providence. The conclusion of this movement would be a combined advance toward Memphis, on the Mississippi, as well as the Memphis and Ohio railroad, and I trust the result would be a glorious one to the country. In a reply to a letter from Gen. Sherman, by the hand of Judge Williams, in relation to the vast importance of securing possession in advance of the country lying between the Ohio, Tennessee, and Mississippi, I have to-day suggested the first part of the preceding plan. By extending my command to Indiana, Tennessee, and Kentucky, you would enable me to attempt the accomplishment of this all-important result; and in order to secure the secresy necessary to its success, I shall not extend the communication which I have made to Gen. Sherman, or repeat it to any one else.

With high respect and regard,

I am, very truly, yours,

J. C. FREMONT.

* This anticipated the rebels a few days, and enabled the United States forces to command the mouth of the Tennesse river.

* Bowling Green was not thus occupied; and was subsequently taken possession of by the rebels, who advanced from it to Muldraugh's Hill, where they threatened Louisville.

† New Madrid was not thus occupied, and has since been held by the rebels; and in the endeavor, months subsequently, to occupy the region opposite Columbus, the disaster of Belmont occurred.

WASHINGTON, D. C.

SCAMMELL & CO., PRINTERS, CORNER OF SECOND & INDIANA AVENUE, THIRD FLOOR.

1862.

CPSIA information can be obtained
at www.ICGtesting.com
Printed in the USA
BVHW011116220219
540827BV00025BA/3160/P